History Mysteries

The Last Tiger

SOLVE ALL THE MYSTERIES!

Solve this wartime mystery and you'll find riches beyond belief . . .

Unravel what happened to the lost explorer and crack a famous cold case . . .

Discover the mystery of de-extinction and create new hope for the Tasmanian tiger . . .

Follow secret clues and buried maps to a legendary treasure of gold . . .

HISTORY MYSTERIES

THE LAST TIGER

MARK GREENWOOD

PUFFIN BOOKS

PUFFIN BOOKS

UK | USA | Canada | Ireland | Australia
India | New Zealand | South Africa | China

Penguin Books is part of the Penguin Random House group of companies whose addresses can be found at global.penguinrandomhouse.com.

Penguin Random House Australia

First published by Penguin Random House Australia Pty Ltd, 2017

1 3 5 7 9 10 8 6 4 2

Cover and text design by Tony Palmer © Penguin Random House Australia Pty Ltd
Cover and internal illustrations © Douglas Holgate
Colour separation by Splitting Image Colour Studio, Clayton, Victoria
Printed and bound in Australia by Griffin Press, an accredited ISO AS/NZS 14001 Environmental Management Systems printer

National Library of Australia Cataloguing-in-Publication entry:
Creator: Greenwood, Mark, author.
Title: The Last Tiger / by Mark Greenwood.

ISBN: 978 0 14 33 0925 3 (paperback)

Series: Greenwood, Mark. History mysteries.
Subjects: Thylacine--Juvenile literature.
Extinct animals--Australia--Juvenile literature.
Natural history--Australia--Juvenile literature.

363.1249099414

Page 8 © 2017 World History Archive / fotoLibra; Page 13 Elias Churchill - (Michael Sharland) Image courtesy The Thylacine Museum; Pages 22/23 Courtesy of The Australian Women's Weekly and The National Library of Australia; Page 30 Courtesy of The Register News-Pictorial / The National Library of Australia, Article 54241041; Pages 44/45 Dave Watts / Alamy Stock Photo Page 54/55 Rosemary Fleay - (David Fleay Natural History Collection) Image courtesy The Thylacine Museum; Page 74 Courtesy of Museums Victoria

penguin.com.au

MIX
Paper from responsible sources
FSC® C009448

For Susan and Michelle

Special thanks to Rosemary Fleay-Thomson; Ken Mulvaney, Principal Advisor, Cultural Heritage, Rio Tinto; Craig Bonney, Chief Executive Officer, Murujuga Aboriginal Corporation; Sean McNeair, Manager, Murujuga Land and Sea Unit; Carol Freeman; Gary Presland, Librarian/ Archivist, Field Naturalists Club of Victoria; Frané Lessac and Michelle Madden

ABOUT MARK

Mark Greenwood is a history hunter. He enjoys searching for lost explorers and glittering treasure, delving into mysteries and solving famous cold cases. Most of all, he loves sharing the stories that he finds.

Mark's books include *Jandamarra* with Terry Denton and *Simpson and his Donkey* with Frané Lessac. His award-winning books about Australia's history have been published around the world.

INTRODUCTION

History tells us that on the evening of 7 September 1936, the last captive Tasmanian tiger died at the Hobart Zoo. It is one of the most famous extinction events in modern history. But is this mysterious marsupial really gone forever?

In the north of Western Australia, I found ancient images of this amazing creature engraved into the rocks of the Burrup Peninsula. These carvings inspired me to find out more about the thylacine and the mystery that surrounds its extinction.

When Europeans came to Australia, they discovered bizarre creatures that couldn't be found anywhere else – the platypus, the echidna, the wombat, the koala and the kangaroo.

The strangest of all was a carnivorous marsupial the size of a large dog with tiger-like stripes. It could hop and leap like a cat and carried its young in a backward-facing pouch.

They called it a wolf, a hyena, a tiger. Its scientific name became *Thylacinus cynocephalus*, meaning 'pouched dog with a wolf's head'.

The thylacine was no stranger to the nation's Aboriginal people. It once roamed all over mainland Australia.

Fossil remains of thylacines have been found in Victoria, South Australia and Queensland.

Its image is painted with ochre on cave walls in the Kimberley and Arnhem Land.

Thousands of years ago Tasmania was part of mainland Australia, until rising sea levels disconnected it from the continent. After thylacines were driven to extinction by disease and competition from the dingo, the last of the species were sealed off on the island.

In the rugged Tasmanian wilderness they ambushed prey on the button-grass plains and coexisted with the Aboriginal people who did not fear or persecute them. In the northeast, they were known as Corinna, the Brave One. The Oyster Bay tribe called them Lagunta.

An ancient engraving of a thylacine from the Burrup Peninsula on mainland Australia

5

In 1642, the Dutch explorer Abel Tasman and his crew stepped ashore and discovered the tracks of an unidentified beast with the paws of a dog and the claws of a tiger.

In the years that followed, sealers and whalers explored the island's windswept shores. French and English expeditions made landfall and sailors reported hearing grunts and snarls and coughing barks. A hideous creature was rumoured to exist in the wild.

In 1805, Lieutenant Governor Paterson filed the first official report of a powerful native carnivore.

Convicts working on chain gangs witnessed curious predators that appeared at night like creatures from a fairytale, staring with shiny black eyes, before loping into the shadows.

As the forests were cleared and the land was fenced, settlers and sheep farmers became fearful of the native tiger. They claimed that its sharp fangs could shear flesh and crush bones. Trappers accused tigers of stealing animals from their snares. Sheep thieves blamed them to disguise their own crimes. Tigers were said to be responsible for attacking flocks, when the culprits were really feral dogs.

Landowners offered rewards to rid their properties of the 'vermin'. A male tiger carcass was worth five shillings. A slain female, with or without young, was worth seven shillings – good money for a poorly paid shepherd.

8

'Either tigers go,' said the farmers, 'or we starve.' In 1888, the Tasmanian Parliament voted to establish a bounty scheme. The financial reward was increased to one pound for each dead tiger.

The extermination of a species had begun . . .

Albert Quarrell with a thylacine killed in December 1911, near Fitzgerald

1
THE TRAPPER

Elias Churchill was a trapper in the wild Florentine Valley. Around his hut, possums and spotted quolls skulked in the darkness. Devils whined and snarled.

On still nights, he used to hear the tigers' husky coughing bark. They would scrounge around for bacon that he left out as bait – but not any more.

It had been twenty-four years since the last tiger bounty had been claimed.

'Tiger Men' used to set cruel traps and slaughter them without pity. In winter, when tiger fur was thick, their skins had fetched a good price for rugs, hats and waistcoats.

Thousands had been hunted and trapped, shot and poisoned. Their skulls hung like trophies on the walls of frontier cabins.

Elias cupped his hands and drank from the mountain stream. He tugged the collar of his jacket up around his ears to shield himself from the morning chill.

The trapper sniffed the air and caught a whiff – a dank odour, unlike any other. 'My oath,' he muttered, 'that's a tiger.'

Elias had lived alone in the wilderness for a long time. He had originally come to the high country to make a living by mining. That barely made enough money for a bag of flour and a tin of jam. Trapping and hunting tigers was a way to survive.

The trapper, Elias Churchill, in 1965, aged 73

Elias found tigers to be timid creatures. He preferred to catch them uninjured. He captured them by suspending a bait over a camouflaged pit. Some tigers gave up without a struggle. Others dropped dead from shock when roped.

Zoos offered good money for live ones. Elias remembered the time he had caught a female and three young pups that had just left the pouch. They were exhibited in country carnivals before he sold them to a zoo.

Tigers were so rare now that this one would fetch a good price. Elias figured he might get twenty pounds – enough money to stock up on supplies.

He followed a trail of blood to the edge of the forest and searched the foliage. 'Ahhh – there you are,' he whispered.

The animal's hind leg was injured. Probably tried to wrench it out of a wire snare, Elias thought.

In the dappled light of the forest, the tiger's eyes were full of fear. It growled and hissed and bared its teeth with a threatening yawn.

Ankle-deep in mud, Elias squelched ever closer to the animal.

'I'm not gunna hurt you,' he whispered.

The wounded animal snarled and backed away. I'll need to handle this fellow with care, thought Elias, or I'll cop a nasty bite.

He held out a leather strap. The tiger arched its back then snapped its jaws around it. Elias pounced on the frightened animal. After a scuffle, he bound its muzzle and paws with rope, and covered its head with a bag. Then he swung the helpless creature over his shoulders and began the long trek home.

It was dark by the time Elias reached his hut. He tied the tiger to a post in the wood shed and offered it fresh wallaby meat. The wounded creature showed no interest. It curled up in a corner and licked its injured paw.

It took a few days before Elias was game enough to enter the wood shed and approach the tiger. It cowered, but the trapper was gentle.

'Ain't you a handsome fella,' he said, softly stroking its back.

The tiger responded to his kindness. Elias ran his hands over its coarse, tawny fur and counted sixteen chocolate-coloured stripes that ran from its shoulder blade to the base of its tail.

Once its leg was on the mend and the tiger was eating, Elias took it by packhorse to the railway station. He loaded it onto a train bound for Hobart Zoo.

Excited children gathered around the guard's van, hoping to catch a glimpse.

'Hey mister,' they said, 'is that a real tiger in there?'

Elias stroked its back.

'Take a good look,' he said. 'It might be the last one you see.'

2
THE WOMAN WHO TAMED TIGERS

Seagulls circled above the tall ships, adding their squabbles to the din on the dock.

Mrs Roberts strode home along the blustery waterfront. On her way, she stopped to chat with friends.

Her husband was a successful businessman and she was a wealthy socialite with a curious hobby. Their house in Hobart – called 'Beaumaris' – was home to many of Tasmania's rarest birds and beasts.

An ever-increasing collection of creatures roamed free in her garden. They hopped and waddled and flew to greet Mrs Roberts when she arrived at the front gate.

She didn't just keep wallabies and ducks, Tasmanian devils and peacocks. Mrs Roberts was well known as ‘the woman who tamed tigers’. She often entered the thylacine cage and sometimes she let the tigers out of their enclosure and walked them around on a lead.

‘Tasmanian tigers are misunderstood,’ she explained. ‘They’re affectionate when I’m with them.’

From time to time, the gardens at Beaumaris were opened up to the public to raise funds for the prevention of cruelty to animals and to promote animal welfare through education.

On Saturdays, Mrs Roberts shared her knowledge of the island’s wildlife with boy scouts and girl guides. She wanted children to know and love the creatures in her private zoo, especially the lesser-known animals and exotic birds that thrived under her care.

Wallabies and possums were her playmates, and she reared Tasmanian devils from the time they were joeys in the pouch.

'I'm possessed by devils,' she joked with the children.

Mrs Roberts wasn't afraid of any of the creatures, 'except the Burmese peacock,' she declared. 'He's such a savage brute.'

She told the children about the persecution of Tasmanian tigers and how she was afraid they would be hunted until none were left.

'These handsome animals are on the brink of extinction,' she said. 'Until we find a sanctuary for them, a zoo is the only option. It might be the only way to save them. At least in a zoo they will be fed and cared for.'

"TIGERS" WERE HER HOBBY

By E. A. BELL

MRS. MARY GRANT ROBERTS feeding some of her flock in a section of her gardens and private zoo in Hobart 70 years ago.

● Whoever heard of women buying, rearing, and selling "tigers?" At the turn of the century a Hobart woman did just that for 15 years. The animal she traded in was the Tasmanian tiger — otherwise known as the marsupial wolf, or thylacine, now almost extinct.

Early Tasmanian zoo enthusiast liked being able to tell her friends that she was also "possessed of seven devils"

Alive still—but elusive

THERE is recent evidence that the "Tasmanian tiger" is not entirely extinct, and zoologists are excitedly awaiting their first chance for more than 30 years to study the animal they have spent thousands of dollars trying to track down.

In 1961 an animal was caught in a trap set by fishermen near Sandy Cape in rugged Western Tasmania; it escaped but left behind blood and hairs which scientists later identified.

For five years there was no further positive evidence that the species still existed. Then a recently used lair was found in rain-forest behind Stanley, on the north-west coast, and again hairs were identified.

Expeditions have been planned, and it is hoped to catch some "tigers" for breeding in captivity.

The scientific name, Thylacinus cynocephalus, meaning "the pouched animal with the wolf head," gives the best brief description. It is about 6ft. from nose to tail-tip, and has been called "tiger" because of the 14 to 16 dark stripes across the brownish yellow body, but "marsupial wolf" is widely adopted as a more appropriate common name, for it is more doglike than cat-like — though the tail is more like a kangaroo's.

The pouch opens backward, and up to four young are reared.

With their fast run and powerful jaws, thylacines hunt down other marsupials, also birds, rabbits, and possibly lizards. They were rarely known to attack man unless cornered or protecting their young.

Trappers used to sell the skins for rugs. The hunt became more vigorous after 1888, when the Government began paying a bounty on their heads. The "tigers," rightly or wrongly, had got a bad name among farmers as killers of sheep and poultry.

Large numbers of thylacines were killed, and by the time the Government decided to protect the species it was all but too late to save it.

Article from the *Australian Women's Weekly*, 1969

The slaughter of tigers finally stopped in 1909, but the damage had been done. Thousands had been exterminated.

Mrs Roberts hired the men who had once been paid to hunt and kill tigers. She offered good money to trappers for live, uninjured animals.

The first tiger she purchased was a female. The second was a mother and three cubs. She tried to look after them and gave them a cage with a separate sleeping den, to protect them from the wind, rain and snow.

'My tigers sleep on straw,' she boasted. 'It keeps their fur in splendid condition.'

The tigers and their playful cubs were star attractions at Beaumaris.

The cubs were nursed on their

mother's milk until they were ready for raw meat, which the butcher delivered every day.

As her private collection grew, zoos from around the world approached Mrs Roberts to purchase the creatures in her care. She sold eagles and hawks, kangaroos, wallabies, possums, parrots, magpies, flying squirrels, echidnas, reptiles and devils.

She had been dealing in tigers for some time – selling them for double the price she paid the trappers. Because they were rare, zoos were willing to pay a high price for healthy specimens – preferably a pair.

Mrs Roberts shipped tigers to Sydney, Melbourne, New York, London, Paris and Berlin. Her hobby had become a successful business.

But no matter how well Mrs Roberts cared for her tigers – no matter how much affection they were shown or what they were fed – when one tiger became sick, the others caught whatever it had, and they all died. Most tigers were restless in captivity and didn't survive more than a few years.

By 1921, when Mrs Roberts was in her seventies, Tasmanian tigers were almost extinct in the wild.

Her private zoo included just one lonely tiger. It paced back and forth in its cage with dark, empty eyes . . .

3
BEAUTY AND THE BEAST

Most children are happy with a pet cat or a dog. Alison Reid preferred lions and leopards.

After Mrs Roberts died suddenly, her collection of birds, marsupials, mammals and reptiles was donated to the Hobart City Council to start a new zoo.

Alison's father was the zookeeper. Seven days a week she helped him, taking tickets at the turnstiles and welcoming visitors.

Alison was only a teenager but she cleaned cages and looked after the baby animals. In the nursery, she reared lion cubs on bottled milk – Betty, Sandy and Susie were playful as kittens. Mike the leopard liked to rumble and tumble, and nibble everything with his sharp, needle-like teeth.

Alison lived with her mother and father in the curator's cottage. All day the young carnivore cubs frolicked in the garden. When Mike the leopard grew bigger, Alison took him for walks around the streets of the Queen's Domain, where the zoo was located.

Mike was always kept on a chain, but his ferocious roar scared the neighbours.

'Don't worry,' Alison assured them. 'Mike won't get up to any tricks when he's with me!'

The zoo bought exotic animals from all over the world. Alison treated them with kindness and affection – whether they were black bears or polar bears, elephants, zebras, meerkats or monkeys.

BEAUTY AND THE BEAST AT THE HOBART ZOO

Girl Whose Greatest Chum Is A Full-Grown Leopard

The average girl is content with a cat or a dog as a pet. Miss Alison Reid, daughter of the curator of the Beaumaris Zoo, at Hobart, prefers a lioness or leopard.

"MY greatest chum in the Zoo is a leopard," she said the other day. "His name is Mike, and he is a great pal. He will be two years' old next August.

"Mike's mother had twins, and—the nasty old thing—she actually ate one of them? So I just had to take charge of the other little fellow to save his life!

"We had a job to get him to take any nourishment at all, but eventually got him accustomed to sucking at a bottle of milk, and fed him just like a baby for six months.

"Then he began to take a fancy to the usual side-lines in the way of food that leopards and lions and tigers like, and made wonderful progress.

"He is a fine chap now—tame, affectionate, and just like a big cat with his playful ways. I still go into his cage regularly to visit him."

When Mike was in the cub stage, Miss Reid used to take him for walks in the Queen's Domain, in which the Zoo is situated, but he was always on a chain, so that he could not play any wild leopard tricks.

Nowadays he is thoroughly accustomed to, and seems to like, his cage home.

"He does not like being taken out of his cage," declared Miss Reid, "and is always anxious to get back. That, to my way of thinking, rather disposes of the idea held by some people that animals in cages must be unhappy.

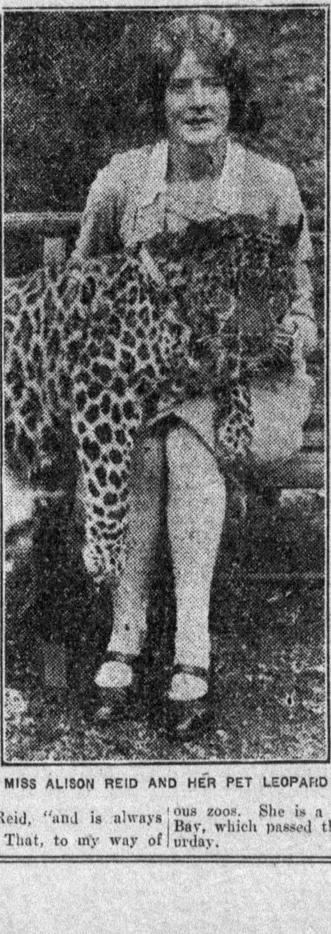

MISS ALISON REID AND HER PET LEOPARD

"Mike knows his name, and will always come when I call him. Strangely enough, he was boisterously rough when a baby, and could use his sharp, needle-like teeth to some order, but now he is as gentle as a lamb.

"I can put my hand in his mouth, and he never bites."

Miss Reid also fostermothered Betty, the only lioness that has been born in the Hobart Zoo.

"Betty's parents were so unkind as to throw her out of the den when she was only a day old," explained Miss Reid. "I took charge of her and reared her. I do not go into her den because Mr. and Mrs. Lion are rather too ferocious, but Betty always knows when I call her and tries to get out.

"Betty is now three, and a big, fine animal."

Miss Reid has reared a lot of pheasants, partridge, and quail, but it is as fostermother of wilder things that she specially excels.

Miss Reid decided a cople of weeks ago to take a trip to England and the Continent, where she plans to see some of the world's most famous zoos. She is a passenger in the Jervis Bay, which passed through Adelaide on Saturday.

Among the creatures inherited from Mrs Roberts was her beloved Tasmanian tiger. Alison visited its cage regularly.

It paced up and down in its reinforced wire enclosure and grew feeble. It pined for freedom and no amount of affection or special care seemed to help.

Sadly, like the others, it died.

It took over a year for Alison's father to find a pair of tigers. But, just as Mrs Roberts had discovered, when one of the tigers became sick, the other caught the illness and they both died.

Newspaper article from
***The Register News – Pictorial*, SA, 1930**

None of the tigers Mr Reid bought survived more than a few years. By 1929, the zoo only had one left – a restless female.

Her coat was in poor condition even though Alison cleaned the cage each morning and coaxed the lonely tiger out of the den. Before dark, she refilled the water bowl and encouraged the tiger back into the sleeping quarters.

'She needs a companion,' Alison told her father.

'I've offered trappers good money,' said Mr Reid, 'but tigers are seldom found in the wild anymore.'

That summer, the Great Depression gripped Australia. Men were unemployed. Families couldn't pay rent. People were forced out of their homes and onto the streets. A day at the zoo was a luxury most people couldn't afford.

Zoo staff were replaced by unemployed men who worked for a voucher for milk and bread. They didn't care about the animals.

Late one Friday night, Alison was woken by a commotion coming from the aviary. There were valuable birds kept there, many of them imported from Africa. She ran downstairs and roused her father.

Mr Reid raced out to find the wire netting had been sliced open. Suddenly an intruder burst out of the shadows, flashing a torch in the zookeeper's face, punching and kicking at him.

Alison's father chased the bird

thief down the dark pathway towards the polar bears' enclosure. When the intruder stumbled and fell, the zookeeper pounced on him.

'Get the police,' Mr Reid yelled out to Alison.

The intruder was long gone by the time Constable Males arrived. Alison guided him along the pathway, sobbing and shaking with fear.

She found her father lying in a pool of blood. His lips were split open by the vicious blows he'd received. His left eye was a swollen lump. His nose and his teeth were broken.

The injuries Alison's father suffered were even worse than first thought. Mr Reid was hospitalised, but he couldn't be saved.

Alison missed him desperately.

Her mother wiped away her tears and tried to console her.

'He'd want you to care for the animals,' she said. 'They still need you.'

Alison took charge of the zoo. She worked seven days a week for no pay – feeding and watering all the animals, making sure they were safe in their sleeping quarters before locking up at night.

In 1933, Alison received exciting news – a male Tasmanian tiger had been captured in the Florentine Valley by a trapper named Elias Churchill. He was on his way to the zoo by rail.

Alison met the train when it arrived in Hobart but was upset to see that the poor creature had a snare wound on his hind leg.

'I found him like that,' said Elias, 'and I looked after him. His leg is on the mend now. If I were you, I wouldn't be too fussy. You might not get another one.'

This tiger showed no sign of ferocity. He seemed quite comfortable in Alison's company. She felt no fear being in the cage with him and the new arrival seemed to get along well with the old female tiger.

But the financial crisis continued to get worse. The city council met to consider the costs of running the zoo.

Alison waited anxiously for the outcome of the meeting. Mr Liscombe, the Superintendent of Reserves, emerged from the council chambers looking grim.

'The zoo might have to close if

things don't improve,' he told her. 'Either way, we will probably have to dispose of the larger animals. And we can't have a woman running the zoo. You and your mother can stay in the cottage, but you'll have to keep working for no pay and hand back the keys to the zoo.'

'At least we still have a roof over our heads,' Alison told her mother. 'There are poor souls sleeping on the streets because of this wretched Depression.'

Early each morning, Alison waited for a council worker to open the zoo gates. She raced about cleaning cages, but the job of inspecting seventy-eight enclosures was too much for one person. Before the gates shut, she did her best to make sure all the animals were in their sleeping quarters.

One day, Alison found the female tiger lying in the corner of the enclosure. Alison stroked the sick tiger – she was having difficulty breathing. Gently, Alison placed her head on the tiger's chest. The wheezing in her lungs was unmistakable.

'Pneumonia,' she whispered.

The female tiger lost weight. Alison put extra straw in the den to make it more comfortable and keep out the chill. She sourced the freshest meat she could find, but the tiger had no appetite.

Despite Alison's best efforts, the poor creature couldn't be saved.

Now there was only one tiger left and the zoo couldn't afford a companion, even if one could be found. The lone tiger clawed at the mesh and paced the enclosure.

The sight of the sullen animal upset the few visitors that still came to the zoo. Children vowed never to return, unless something was done for the tiger.

Alison pleaded, again and again, for the keys so she could look after the animals after hours. The Town Clerk and Mr Liscombe denied her requests.

'They don't think a girl can do the work,' Alison told her mother. 'But the cages are filthy and some animals haven't been fed. There's only one tiger left and if he's not put in his den at night he has no protection when the weather turns icy.'

In September 1936, the night-time

temperatures plummeted to freezing. The days were unseasonably hot. Sick, neglected animals paced their enclosures. The once-mighty black panther caught pneumonia and died.

Alison tried to reason with Mr Liscombe. 'The leaves have fallen from the tree that shades the tiger's cage,' she said. 'The poor thing is exposed to the sun all day and sometimes the workers forget to put him in his den for the night. He won't survive if something isn't done.'

Instead of helping, Mr Liscombe made Alison's life even more miserable. 'I'm afraid the zookeeper's cottage is no longer available. You and your mother have one week to find shelter elsewhere.'

In her final week in the cottage,

Alison listened helplessly to the tiger's agitated, coughing bark and the distress calls of the other animals as they faced another freezing night.

She sat on the end of her bed and sobbed. The tiger's *yip yip yap* had become more of a whimper than a bark.

He's locked out of his den again, she thought. But there was nothing Alison could do . . .

4
BENJAMÍN

In a pen near the rear gate of the Hobart Zoo, the last captive tiger paced up and down.

These days people refer to the last tiger as Benjamin, but that wasn't what Alison called him. The name comes from the recollections of a man who falsely claimed to have worked at the zoo. Over the years the name was repeated so often it was accepted.

By the early 1930s, Tasmanian tigers were highly endangered. The Animals and Birds Protection Board expressed their concern about this rare species and David Fleay, a respected scientist and zoologist, came to Hobart to study the last tiger in captivity.

He filmed haunting images of an unhappy animal pacing in its barren cage.

A still from the film of Benjamin, the last Tasmanian tiger in captivity, taken by David Fleay in 1933

It would be the last footage taken of a Tasmanian tiger, a species now very close to extinction. The grainy black-and-white images are some of the only film we have of a living Tasmanian tiger.

In those days, cameras were not light and small as they are today. Fleay had to focus the camera with his head under a black cloth. He didn't notice that the tiger had crept behind him. But he certainly felt it when Benjamin bit him on the bum.

Fleay suffered no serious injury – in fact he regarded Benjamin's bite as a compliment and declared it 'the highlight of my natural history career'.

Filming the last captive tiger fuelled Fleay's desire to do what he could to save the species. He applied for permission to capture a pair in order to breed them in a wildlife sanctuary. But because of the Great Depression, funds were not available to mount an expedition.

It took another three years before the Governor of Tasmania bowed to mounting pressure to legally protect Tasmanian tigers.

A declaration was signed, but it was too late for Benjamin.

Exposed to the elements night and day, with no access to shelter, the last tiger curled up in a cold corner of the cage. On the evening of 7 September 1936, Benjamin closed his eyes and died.

The body was forwarded to the Hobart Museum, but the coat was in such poor condition that no attempt was made to preserve it.

Benjamin's body was tossed into the bin.

5
TIGER TALES

When the Hobart Zoo first opened in 1923, newspapers sang its praises as a 'playground for animals'. The grounds reverberated to the roar of panthers and the screeches of spider monkeys. Polar bears splashed in a narrow moat. An elephant trundled along the pathway with giggling children on its back.

By 1937, the zoo was in a terrible state and no new buyer could be found. One year after Benjamin's death, Alison's much-loved lions were shot.

Today the old zoo site is fenced off and overgrown. The crumbling concrete ruins are the only reminder of the cramped enclosures. It is known as the place where the last Tasmanian tiger died.

But was Benjamin the last tiger? Did the entire species become extinct on that bleak night?

The Tasmanian wilderness is vast. Could tigers still exist in areas that remain uninhabited?

In 1938, the first official search was organised by the Tasmanian Animals and Birds Protection Board. The expedition was led by local bushmen, under the command of a police inspector.

Traps failed to secure a tiger, but tiger prints were found. Plaster cast impressions of footprints taken at Jane River confirmed that Tasmanian tigers were still living in the wild at that time.

Journeys into 'Tiger Country' are not for the faint-hearted, even now. Search parties have to endure mosquitos, leeches, ticks and the threat of venomous snakes. Tiger hunters must cross swollen rivers and trek through boggy swamps. They must brave freezing rain and treacherous conditions.

In November 1945, David Fleay was determined to try to secure a male and female tiger, alive and unharmed for breeding. He'd successfully bred many species in captivity, including the platypus. He feared the threat of thylacine extinction was nearing its final phase.

In a last-ditch attempt to preserve the tigers, Fleay set off into the wilderness, accompanied by his young family. Eight-year-old Rosemary became her father's trusty helper.

The Fleay family leapt across swift-running creeks. They trekked through dark, dripping forests and hiked along moss-covered riverbanks.

Rosemary learned how to set up wire-framed traps, with doors that dropped after an animal tugged at the bait. Old bushmen said tigers used to lick frying pans used for cooking bacon so Rosemary singed meat on the campfire then laced it with oil of aniseed '. . . to attract tigers to the traps like bees to a honey pot.'

It was her task to lay the bait trails. She wandered alone for kilometres in dense bush, dragging bacon on a string in every direction, to and from the traps.

At a safe distance, the Fleay family set up camp and waited for the nocturnal tigers to appear.

A photo taken by David Fleay in 1945 of Rosemary setting traps in south-west Tasmania

Rosemary and her brothers huddled under a canvas tent to shelter from storms and freezing rain.

'It was blazing hot one day,' Rosemary tells people who ask, 'and the next day we huddled under our canvas tent to shelter from storms and freezing rain. Floods often washed us out. Our camp was mud and slush – and always invaded by snakes. Mornings were the most exciting times. We raced to our "catch-em-alive" traps, hoping for a tiger. But we only found native cats and spotted quolls and devils gnawing on the wire.'

Rosemary's father led the search, over snowy peaks and across icy mountain streams.

On Poverty Plain, the aurora australis danced in the southern sky like a curtain of rainbow-coloured light.

'Three times during the night, my father said he heard a sound unlike the call of any animal or bird he'd ever heard,' Rosemary says. 'He was sure it was a tiger's voice.'

The next morning, she found scuffled tracks that resembled the prints of a tiger. Plaster casts were taken. Rosemary collected animal poo scats, hoping to find evidence of a tiger, while her father inspected the trap and carefully gathered some fur caught in the wire.

'He was certain it belonged to a tiger that got away,' Rosemary said.

Later, the Tasmanian Museum inspected the fur, scats and prints. They concluded that it was possible they had come from a Tasmanian tiger, but that was never proven.

After weeks in the wilderness, everyone was tired. Food supplies were low and Rosemary's father could not afford to stay away from work any longer. He tried to hide his disappointment.

'All that hard work for nothing,' he sighed.

'Just because we didn't see one or capture one,' Rosemary reassured her father, 'doesn't mean they don't exist . . .'

6
SIGHTINGS

Academics and scientists from all over the world have taken up the study of Tasmanian tigers and devoted years of their lives to the striped marsupial carnivore.

Conservationists and naturalists have joined the crusade to find out whether tigers still exist in the wild, and the elusive creature has enthralled writers, artists and filmmakers.

The 1938 expedition that found tracks at Jane River proved that at least one tiger was still alive in the wild after Benjamin died. The plaster impressions of the tiger claws and pads they found are on display at the Tasmanian Museum.

Since then, other alleged tiger tracks have been found, but the casts are incomplete so no one can prove that they came from a tiger.

No hair samples or scats have returned DNA that matches that of the Tasmanian tiger.

Without a living creature or a body for examination, the case for extinction is strong – yet many people continue to claim they have seen a living tiger.

In 1957, a striped animal resembling a Tasmanian tiger was spotted on a deserted beach from a helicopter, but an expedition sent to the area failed to locate the animal.

Attacks on sheep were investigated in the 1960s, after reports of tiger sightings in the Florentine Valley. The havoc turned out to be the work of wild dogs.

In 1980, a woman claimed to have come face to face with a tiger sniffing around her chicken coop. She called out to her husband, but the striped creature disappeared into the woods.

'It was so serene and trusting,' she told reporters. 'It didn't look like it was in a hurry. No wonder they got killed.'

An old bushman called Bert was reportedly feeding tigers on his property in the Weld Valley in 1993.

'It went eerily quiet one night,' he said. 'Even the dogs were still. From my window I could see a tiger near the chook house. It just stood there sniffing the air. I reckon it picked up my scent. It came back the following day with a female and two young pups. I started feeding them . . . and they kept coming back.'

These are just some of the thousands of sightings that have steadily increased every year, but still no one has conclusive photographic evidence.

In 1982, one of the most reliable reports was kept secret while an extensive search was conducted.

At the time, the sighting was described as 'irrefutable' and 'conclusive'. It was taken seriously because the witness was a respected ranger with the Tasmanian Parks and Wildlife Service.

Hans Naarding was asleep in his four-wheel drive, deep in the bush in north-west Tasmania. He worked in remote locations so he could study migratory birds and nocturnal wildlife.

Around 2am, he was woken by the pouring rain. Out of habit, the ranger opened his window to shine a spotlight around.

'As I scanned the surrounds,' he said, 'the beam came to rest on a large tiger standing side-on in front of the vehicle, six to seven metres away.'

The animal stood perfectly still and stared into the light. With his camera out of reach, the ranger thought it best to note every detail.

'It was the size of a large dog,' he said, 'with a unique head and a stiff tail. At one point, it yawned and its teeth were clearly visible.'

Hans estimated its weight and counted twelve stripes on its sandy coat.

'It was a male,' he said, 'in excellent condition.'

After observing the animal for three minutes, Hans tried to get a photo.

'I pulled my arm back in to reach for my camera, but in doing so I disturbed the tiger. He turned and ambled into the thick undergrowth.'

The ranger quickly wriggled out of his sleeping bag and went after the tiger. He searched for footprints, but the rain had washed away the tracks.

'I recognised a strong odour,' he said. 'It reminded me of hyenas in Africa.'

The next morning, colleagues at the Tasmanian National Parks and Wildlife Service were alerted.

Hans was told to stay where he was while other rangers raced to the scene, hoping to verify the presence of a tiger.

Officers searched a two-hundred-and-fifty kilometre area. Road kill was put out as bait. Cameras were set up along the river and in areas where sand and mud might capture tracks. Animal scats were collected and 'possible' tracks were found.

The Tasmanian National Parks and Wildlife Service kept the sighting secret from the public for nearly two years.

When the news finally broke, Hans was overwhelmed by requests from around the world to speak on radio and television.

After this sighting, a Thylacine Response Kit was created to ensure proper collection of evidence.

The sighting-report form scores

tiger observations based on light and weather conditions, along with the length of time the animal was observed, the reliability of the person who made the sighting and whether they were alone at the time.

Thylacines were officially declared extinct in 1986 and the Tasmanian Parks and Wildlife Service considers that the species is gone forever. They no longer search for tigers.

Since then, more than four thousand sightings have been reported and it's highly likely that there are many more.

Some people keep quiet for fear of being ridiculed. Others say nothing because they believe publicity could place the tiger in danger.

'If you see a tiger,' locals say, 'don't tell anyone.'

Modern investigators use night-vision cameras, motion sensors and four-wheel drives to enter rugged terrain. They set traps near overhangs and rocky outcrops – the sites of possible tiger lairs. In difficult country, helicopters are sometimes used to fly in supplies and equipment.

Tasmanian tiger sightings since 1936

N
W
E
S

After so many searches, it appears that the tiger is truly extinct. But is there another way to meet a tiger?

7
TEST TUBE TIGERS

What if extinction was curable?

'Resurrection science' was once considered an impossible dream – something out of science fiction. But scientists are constantly pushing the frontiers of research in genetics and evolutionary biology. One day, they hope to revive, restore and reintroduce an extinct species.

Sheep, pigs and mice have already been cloned. Why not create an identical copy of a Tasmanian tiger?

Some scientists believe that the impossible dream of de-extinction may be less than twenty years away.

It all depends on DNA, the code that contains genetic information. It is found in the cells of living organisms.

DNA contains instructions about

how we grow and behave and what we look like. Just as the letters in the alphabet can be put together to form a word or a sentence, DNA is put together to form cells and ultimately living things.

To clone a Tasmanian tiger, scientists would have to create a 'library' of tens of thousands of genes. The DNA from each cell is required for cloning (along with a lot of other tricky scientific things).

In 1999, the Australian Museum launched a program to bring a Tasmanian tiger back to life. They hoped to use DNA taken from a preserved tiger pup.

After more than one hundred and fifty years of being pickled in alcohol, the pup's DNA had deteriorated.

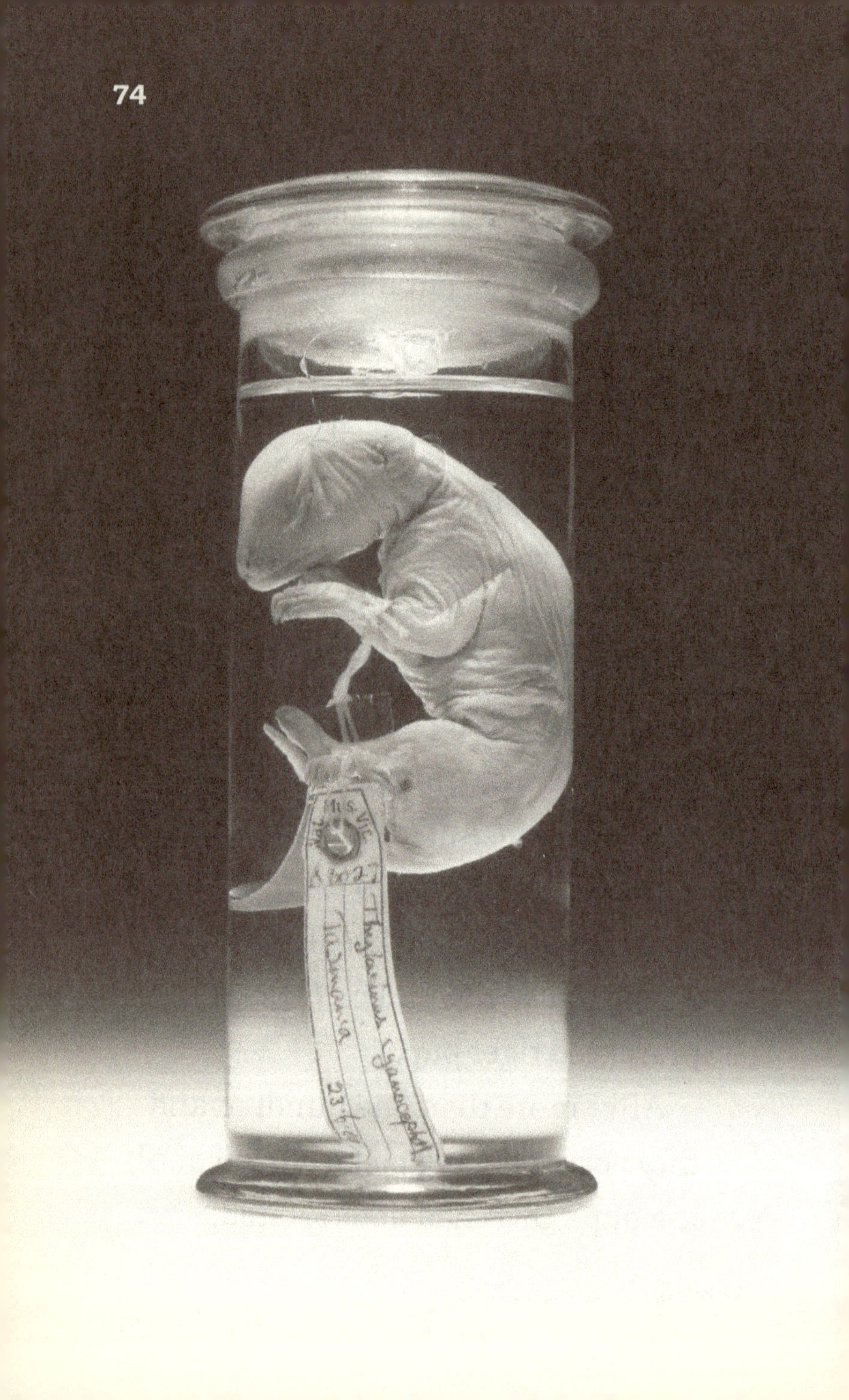

It was contaminated by microorganisms and fungus growing on its skin.

The museum finally cancelled the thylacine cloning program after years of trying.

Even if, against the odds, tiger DNA could be successfully extracted, how would a pup be born? The cells would need to be transferred into the cell of another animal.

Without a living Tasmanian tiger, scientists would need to find a substitute mother from a related species.

A thylacine pup preserved in alcohol since 1866

The closest living relative is the Tasmanian devil. What would be the result of combining a tiger and a devil?

Scientists can't clone an extinct animal just yet. It's still a dream. But is restoring any extinct species a good thing? Or should we leave things as they are?

Many people are against cloning. They believe nature shouldn't be interfered with. Others argue that humans exterminated tigers and therefore we have a responsibility to bring them back to life.

Living creatures are much more than just DNA put together in a laboratory. Would cloned tigers be displayed as public entertainment in zoos – or released into the wilderness?

Would they be sold? Who would own them?

Just as the sale of the original tigers made Mrs Roberts a lot of money, the market for cloned tigers would surely become big business.

8
EXTINCTION

National Threatened Species Day is observed every 7 September – a date that commemorates Benjamin's death. It is a day to reflect on how we can protect the rarest wildlife species on earth.

Tragically, Australia has many critically endangered species and one of the highest extinction rates in the world. The story of the Tasmanian tiger reminds us how important it is to conserve threatened flora and fauna.

The thylacine became an animal to fear and exterminate because of human ignorance and the idea of progress. 'There is not one redeeming point in the cowardly animal,' farmers declared. 'It is worthless, except for its hide.'

Now human memory of the

Tasmanian tiger is preserved only in ancient rock art, dog-eared photographs and drawings, the memories of old bushmen and sixty-two seconds of silent black-and-white film. The pickled pup and thylacine fossils are exhibited with skulls, bones and skins in museums and private collections.

The tiger, once real, is now only imagined. This once-despised animal now features on the coat of arms of Tasmania. It is the logo of a city, a TV station, a supermarket, a bus line and a cricket team. It is the subject of feature films, documentaries, artworks and books.

I cling to a faint hope that somewhere in the wilderness the Tasmanian tiger lives on. Scientific evidence suggests otherwise and there is no conclusive proof, but there's plenty of unexplored tiger country.

In recent years, a different kind of bounty has been put on the Tasmanian tiger. In the 1980s, an American businessman put up $100,000 as an incentive to find one in the wild. Then a magazine offered $1.25 million to capture a live, uninjured animal. A travel company topped that with an offer of $1.75 million. But proof that this wonderful creature still exists would be priceless . . .

Are you a true believer? Could *you* be the one to rediscover the tiger? Or perhaps one day you'll be the scientist who goes down in history for bringing a tiger back from the dead.

THE STORY OF HISTORY

When the comparatively small island of Tasmania becomes more densely populated, and its primitive forests are intersected with roads . . . the numbers of this animal will speedily diminish . . . and it will then be recorded as an animal of the past – John Gould, 1851

This story began with two very different artworks, each containing evidence of the thylacine: petroglyphs (ancient Aboriginal rock art) from the Dampier Archipelago on the Australian mainland, and sixty-two precious seconds of silent black-and-white film from Tasmania.

Made four thousand years apart, these cultural artefacts preserve the memory of an animal now lost. They were the inspiration behind this book.

You'll find a list of events in the timeline and recommended reading on the More to Explore page to help you further investigate this history mystery!

TIMELINE OF EVENTS

43,000 ago Tasmania is joined to mainland Australia by a land bridge.

10,000–12,000 years ago Tasmania is separated from the Australian mainland by rising sea levels.

3000–4000 years ago Thylacine images are etched into rocks on the Burrup Peninsula, in the Pilbara region of Western Australia.

2000–3000 years ago The thylacine is extinct on mainland Australia.

1642 Abel Tasman's crew find tracks of an unusual animal.

1772–1802 French and British sailors make landfall in south-east Tasmania.

1803–4 British forces occupy Risdon Cove.

1804 Escaped convicts report seeing a large tiger.

1805 Leiutenant Governor Paterson files the first official report of a powerful native carnivore.

1807 First scientific description of the thylacine.

1809 The Parisian zoologist E Geoffroy Saint-Hilaire assigns the Tasmanian tiger to the genus Dasyurus, along with marsupial quolls.

1817 The colonists begin to stock Tasmania with sheep to develop a wool export business.

1824 Thylacines suspected of killing sheep.

1824 Conrad Jacob Temminck creates the genus name, *Thylacinus cynocephalus.*

1830 The first thylacine bounty is introduced by the Van Diemen's Land Company.

1836 'Tiger men' are appointed.

1840 The second bounty scheme begins.

1842 Settlers report a decline in tiger numbers.

1850 First prediction of thylacine extinction is reported to the Zoological Society of London.

1863 Thylacines are rarely seen and the species is considered threatened. Naturalist John Gould predicts their extinction.

1887 Van Diemen's Land Company bounty scheme pays out for seventy thylacine kills.

1888 The Tasmanian Parliament enacts another thylacine bounty – 1 pound per adult animal 'destroyed', 10 shillings for every pup.

1895 Mrs Roberts' Beaumaris Zoo opens to the public.

1909 The government bounty scheme is terminated after 2184 bounties are paid.

1908 Mary Roberts purchases her first thylacine – an adult female.

1910 Thylacines are considered rare and are sought after by zoos around the world.

1921 Mrs Roberts dies.

1923 Beaumaris Zoo animals are relocated to the Queen's Domain and the Hobart Zoo is opened under the care of Arthur Reid.

1926 London Zoo purchases its last thylacine.

1933 The last tiger is trapped in the Florentine Valley and sold to the Hobart Zoo.

1933 The last captive tiger is filmed by naturalist David Fleay.

1936 Tasmanian government places thylacines on the protected list.

1936 The last captive tiger dies of exposure on 7 September.

1938 An expedition makes casts of tiger prints found at Jane River.

1973 The Australian government bans all thylacine exports.

1986 The Tasmanian tiger is officially declared extinct by international standards.

1999 A thylacine cloning project launched by the Australian Museum begins.

2005 The Australian Museum halts the project to clone the thylacine due to the DNA being too degraded to construct a 'DNA library'.

MORE TO EXPLORE

Websites

www.naturalworlds.org/thylacine

http://circuszooanimals.blogspot.com.au/search?q=tasmanian+tiger

https://www.youtube.com/watch?v=sjOKamE1pgo

publications.rzsnsw.org.au/doi/pdf/10.7882/AZ.2008.024

Newspaper articles online

Advocate, Friday 22 June 1945
trove.nla.gov.au/newspaper/article/68929303?

Examiner, Friday 19 February 1937
trove.nla.gov.au/newspaper/article/52124921

Books

Freeman, Carol. *Paper Tiger*. Forty South Publishing, 2014

Guiler, E. R. *Tasmanian Tiger: A lesson to be learnt*. Abrolhos Publishing, 1998.

Owen, David. *Thylacine: The Tragic Tale of the Tasmanian Tiger*. Allen & Unwin, 2011.